The Moses Principle of Leadership:

TEACH, TELL AND TRAIN

BY

STANLEY G. BUFORD

DEDICATION

This book is Dedicated to all the hard-working families that make books like "The Moses Principle" possible.

Proceeds from this book will go to the From Boys to Men Network

A 501(C) (3) Non-Profit Foundation

Stanley G. Buford, Executive Director
7115 West North Avenue
Suite 163
Oak Park, IL 60302

fromboystomen@gmail.com

The Moses Principle of Leadership:
Teach, Tell & Train

TriDreams Productions

Copyright © 2017/2025 by Stanley G. Buford

Buford, Stanley G

This publication is designed to provide accurate and authoritative information regarding the subject matter covered. It is sold under the understanding that the publisher is not engaged in rendering legal, accounting, or other professional services. If legal advice or other expert assistance is required, the services of a competent professional person should be sought.

It's an E-book, it's an Audiobook, it's a fantastic song; TriDreams Productions, and you won't go wrong! ®

Other Books by Author Stanley G. Buford

[Bick & Stink Meet King Solomon (Tales Of Bible Characters:21st Century)](#)

- 2 Editions
- Average Review: ★★★★★

[Encounter With An Angel: He Always Paved My Way](#)

- 2 Editions
- Average Review: ★★★★★

[Far Away: Love Has No Bounds](#)

- Kindle Edition
- Average Review: ★★★★★

[The Fragile Angel](#)

- 2 Editions
- Average Review: ★★★★★

[Good Advice...Is Just That!](#)

- 2 Editions
- Average Review: There are no reviews yet

[Grace & Grant Find The Open Door](#)

- Kindle Edition
- Average Review: ★★★★★

Growing Up Poor In A Frank lloyd Wright Home

- 2 Editions
- Average Review: 

I'm Waiting For A Miracle!

- Kindle Edition
- Average Review: 

Kids in the Kitchen

- Kindle Edition
- Average Review: There are no reviews yet

Nine Pounds of Gold (Adventures of Bick & Stink Book 2)

- 2 Editions
- Average Review:

AUTHORS NOTE TO READERS:

It is the ultimate achievement of every kingdom groundbreaker: to be the least, the last, and the lowliest leader. One must fulfill their assignment within the borders of lonely leadership or insensitive reaction to that leadership; wise men like Solomon, Apostle Paul, and Moses were described in their lifespans as prophets who, at times, commanded no respect. If you seek leadership, know you are requesting an existence of service and loneliness. It is not at all times a glamorous service; rather, it is desolate and lonely. This writer has studied the book of Proverbs for years and is only beginning to scratch the surface of what the Bible teaches about wisdom with a view to leadership.

Leadership is the prospect of staring, face to face, with a crew with no direction and no plan, depending on you to lead the way. Leadership is choosing between equally undesirable alternatives. It is holding the worries of others on your shoulder while you go unnoticed. It may be a life of discreet prayer. Sometimes, it seems as though you are choosing between being liked in competition with being respected. You may find consolation behind a pulpit, as a Pastor, which is arguably one of the loneliest jobs in town, all things being equal. Strong leadership skills can be good for a career but will inevitably trade-off with emotional support. For many talented men and women, this *"call to service"* consequently promotes its qualities which can then be turned into assets that are used to secure and maintain certain types of services to mankind. In almost any career field or industry, there will be professions that require the ability to lead others and inspire them with motivational, measured and team-building maneuvers. This book was fashioned in order to address this need. Although written from a Christian perspective, its wisdom can be used across the varied gender, religious, age, ideological, political and geographical spectrums. If you aspire to manage people, no matter what your background, this book is must-read. Thank you for your purchase...Enjoy!

FOREWORD

Stanley G. Buford was born in Chicago, Illinois. His paternal DNA attests to the fact that he shares patriarchal genetic ancestry with the Akan people of Ghana on the continent of Africa. Today, he resides in the Village of Oak Park, Illinois. As an undergraduate student, Mr. Buford studied at Illinois State University and now holds two master's degrees- one from National-Louis University in Management/Human Resource Development and one from DePaul University in Curriculum Development. He has worked as a teacher and parent coordinator in the Chicago Public Schools for over 15 years, where he was designated the "Trainer of Trainers" for the Character Development Curriculum by the Programs Director, Dr. Leon Hendricks. He has especially been delighted in writing ***"The Moses Principle of Management: Teach, Tell & Train"*** for a number of personal and professional reasons. He has appeared as a guest speaker on the nationally televised show, "Heartbeat of America," in a frank discussion concerning institutional challenges to climbing the corporate and educational ladders.

Buford owns and operates a state-certified management consulting business, Terkat Consultants Inc. He has been quoted in a variety of news articles while lecturing at schools such as Blackburn University, Northwestern, DePaul, University of Illinois and The Chicago Consortium of Colleges and Universities on a variety of contemporary issues. Stanley is a successful freelance journalist and is a contributor and staff writer for three national publications. He has authored over 25 non-fiction, fiction, self-help and children's books, which the nation's top 5 retailers have sold: Barnes & Noble, eBay, Target, Wal-Mart, and Amazon.com. Remarkably, the book ***"Not All Teachers Are Parents, But All Parents Are Teachers"*** was publicly endorsed by President Barack Obama as: "[an] interesting book on parenting."

Mr. Buford, having served as President of the Phi Beta Sigma Fraternity-Upsilon Sigma Chapter in Chicago and Vice President for Programs of the Phi Delta Kappa Fraternity's joint University of Chicago/DePaul University Chapter; is no stranger to Leadership and Management, and has served as the Program Director of the School Partnerships Program, a school improvement project at DePaul University's Center for Urban Education. Stanley retains the designation of Professor at the renowned Black Star Parent University, Chicago, Illinois, teaching a variety of parenting classes to eager adults for the past 10 years. He has also served as an adjunct faculty member at Concordia University, where his predisposition is in teaching his favorite class: ***Management of Organizational Systems***. He is a recipient of 2 National Leadership Awards in Business during his years in corporate America. He has also been awarded the prestigious "Keeping America Strong" Award presented by actor William Shatner. Mr. Buford started a mentoring program (From Boys to Men Network Foundation) in 1991, which seeks to improve the quality of life for school-age boys on Chicago's west side. He is an actor, playwright, marathoner, visionary and doting father.

Ordained into Christian ministry in 1992 with a kick-off sermon for our times: ***"Leading by Example,"*** he presently works in ministry as liaison to Pastor Mark A.

Henton in the Monument of Faith Evangelistic Church in Chicago, Illinois. In addition, he has served as a teacher in the Children's Church and also assists the Director in the organization and administration of the Big Brothers Mentoring Program as a Parent Advocate. In this role, he organizes and oversees parent group leaders, as well as developing an academic and social enrichment curriculum. At the same time, he has served as the president of the Men's Department at Monument; appointed in 2007 by Apostle Richard D. Henton. In this vital role, he sponsors workshops and seminars presented by leaders and management specialists in an attempt to equip designated individuals with the ability to assist with community development from within and outside the church, school, community and family. Prior to his membership at Monument, Stanley served for 12 years in various capacities as a Sunday school teacher, New Members Class Coordinator, Youth Director and Assistant Pastor under the leadership of the late and renowned Evangelist E. R. Allen at the Christ Bible Center Church in Chicago, Illinois. To the youth leaders of America, he has a simple philosophy to deliver- ***Say what you mean, and mean what you say!***

Stanley has touched the lives of students across varied age, ideological, political and geographical spectrums, as evidenced by a conversation he had years ago with an aspiring writer he conversed with via Facebook after she read an article he had penned as a staff writer of a national magazine describing the "6 P's" of Leadership: ***Proper Preparation and Planning Prevents Poor Performance;*** to which she inquired: "I want to be a writer too! I am an undergraduate student at the Rivers State University in Port Harcourt, Nigeria. I write poems and stories; can you be my mentor/coach?" Stanley naturally accepted as he and Lilian Okosi are good friends and contemporaries today, thanks to that happenstance.

Another profound example of a youth leader he worked with was a 17-year-old freelance writer from Boston named Yuhang Zhang. Stanley first contacted him for some assistance and advice on editing an article for his non-profit group; within the span of a conversation, Yuhang decided to work pro bono as an intern/volunteer for Stanley's "From Boys to Men Network Foundation"; a 501 © 3 organization. Over a year, they worked together on various projects involving social justice and racial issues in America, notably including the process of organizing a meeting with Pope Francis to discuss police brutality in the summer of 2015. Stanley is immensely grateful for the assistance provided by Yuhang but also happy that he could provide opportunities, confidence and advice to this future business leader whose sights are set on his continued progression as a student at Harvard University in the fall.

Throughout his life, Stanley has inspired young leaders like yours truly to understand and leverage the power of education. I know this better than anyone; I happen to be his daughter. Having the foresight and belief in a strong academic foundation, my father, by way of homeschooling, taught me to read at the age of 3. I earned my Ph.D. in sociology from the University of Maryland, with a concentration in social theory and international/historical sociology. I wrote my dissertation on cultural entrepreneurship inspired by one of Dad's key lessons to myself and my sibling Terrence: ***Be your own boss, and you will control your destiny***. I hope that through this book, ***The Moses Principle of Leadership: Teach, Tell***

and Train, you, the reader/leader, will experience what I had the privilege of experiencing growing up.

Kathryn C. Buford, Ph.D.

MecLabs Institute Certified,

President/Chief Executive Officer and

Founder, Watershed

Chicago, Illinois

Thank you to the leaders who have influenced my life with words of wisdom & support:

To my loving mother, Juanita Buford-Puckett, for teaching me to always remember:

"Treat people the way you want to be treated."

______________________Clergy______________________

Pastor Mark Anthony Henton: "Everything around you is getting better!"

Apostle Richard Daniel Henton: "Don't be surprised at what God will do with [your] hands!"

Pastor E. R. Allen: "God is turning it around for your good!"

Dr. Margret White: "Never hesitate to tell a young person, by way of your testimony, how God has educated you for His glory and purpose. It may just be the inspiration they need to live by!"

My friend Pastor Joseph Allen-Roe: (humorously): "Stanley...keep looking up!" ☺

Rev. R. W. Schaumbach: "You don't have any trouble; all you need is faith in God!

My mentor in the Gospel: Apostle Louis Greenup: "Repeat after me...I'll never be broke another day in my life."

Prophecy of Evangelist Sister Ann when I was 7 years old: "Hmmm; This young man's gonna be a preacher someday!"

______________Education/Business/Government______________

Mr. H. Craig Jones: My former H. S. teacher, mentor, friend and fraternity brother: "You can and should stand out among men!"

Dr. Hazel Loucks; Ill. Deputy Gov. for Ed. & Workforce Development: "We are looking forward to using programs like your From Boys to Men Network within [Illinois] schools in order to prevent school violence. Governor George Ryan and I wish you much success."

State Sen. Kimberly A. Lightford: "I support the work of Stanley G. Buford in the public and private sector in his quest to assist business and educational entities in the State of Illinois."

Mayor Harold Washington: "I congratulate you on your past accomplishments and look forward to your continued contributions to our community."

Congressman Danny K. Davis: "I want you to help me bring professionals to the table that will help our communities deal with solutions to the problems that we face today."

Mr. John Swearingen, CEO-Standard Oil of Indiana; CINB: "Stan, you have to treat your family's economics the same way you would a company's economy, as if it were your own!"

President William Jefferson Clinton: "All Americans should be able to rise as far as their God-given talents and determination can take them. As we continue our work toward that goal, I am grateful for your involvement."

President Barack Obama: "Thank you for [an] interesting book on parenting" (Not All Teachers Are Parents, But All Parents Are Teachers!")

Tusuneo Ohiouye; CEO-Mitsubishi Mfg. Of America: "We have taken proactive steps to reinforce Mitsubishis' diversity efforts... [should] we have a need in the future, we will consider Terkat."

Ricardo C. Dizon, M. D.: We are pleased to have Stanley G Buford, President/CEO of Terkat Consultants Inc., as Director of Marketing for our Home Services Medical Division.

Will Robinson, first Black head coach at an NCAA Division I School (Illinois State University): "Keep your head up champ; I'm going places, and you're with me!"

Edyth E. Young, Ph.D.; NCREL: I have known Mr. Buford for years, and he has never wavered in his commitment to education and helping our youth. His ability to interact with students and their parents, administrators, community leaders, and government officials is extraordinary and poised.

_____________________Book Reviews_____________________

Les Brown: "Your new book is awesome; [Not All Teachers Are Parents, But All Parents Are Teachers!]"

Shana Rose, Selena You're Beautiful! 5 Star review (Amazon.com): "Buford makes a convincing point with his main characters: Never give up on the power and the will of the human spirit to heal and move forward."

Vernita Naylor, The Fragile Angel, 5 Star review (Readers Favorite): "[This] is a wonderful short story that includes a poem that helps to illustrate the unconditional love of God. Stanley has created this story in English, French and Spanish, which gives it a beautifully international touch".

Mamta Madhavan, Winners Never Quit, and Quitters Never Win! 5 Star Review (Readers Favorite): "It's a good bedtime storybook and can also be used for read-aloud sessions in classrooms and school libraries. All educators, counselors, and parents will find the tips and suggestions given by author [Stanley G Buford] useful on how to handle the problem of bullying".

Simeon Wright (Cousin to civil rights icon-Emmett Till): It has most certainly been a pleasure for me to write the Foreword for your most recent children's book. Thanks, Dad! I wish you great success!

LEADING BY EXAMPLE IN AN ORGANIZATION

1. Do I model patience?
2. Do I wear appropriate attire that exemplifies a professional image?
3. Do I model punctuality?
4. Do I comment promptly and appropriately on work performance gone wrong to my team?
5. Do I give individual comments that are designed to motivate participants to excel?
6. Do I treat participants with impartially with no suggestion of favoritism?
7. Do I maintain compassion and calmness even in stressful scenarios?
8. Do I refrain from responding to negative chatter about group leaders in my charge?
9. Have I attempted to communicate positive news to those involved with the team effort?
10. Do I model humility in a caring/winning attitude with a smile?
11. Am I familiar with the community, in which my organization is located?
12. Do I refrain from talking negatively about peers/coworkers in the common areas of the organization I represent.

If you answered **no** to any item above in your leadership capacity continue to read this book.

Table of Contents

CHAPTER 1
The Moses Principle of Leadership

Teach

Many times, we are told that the Holy Bible has answers to most of the questions that plague us. Certainly, this is very true when it comes to leadership principles. I have been fortunate to implement, as a leader, sometimes by default in the educational, business and political realm of society, some of these Biblical-based principles. I know what leadership is because, in many cases, I have been forced to "follow" or ply leadership principles upon a stumbling block and then turn it into a steppingstone rather than viewing it as a hindrance. I have never been an avid fan of testing. I have never tested well in my K-12 years of academia. An 8th-grade counselor once told my mother while explaining/interpreting the results of my ITBS (Iowa Test of Basic Skills) scores, "Stanley will never be 'book smart' or academically inclined beyond his grade school years." Mrs. Anderson said emphatically, to which my mother responded: "He said he wanted to go to college someday; you don't think that's possible for him?" my mother queried. "Oh no...Put him in a vocational or trade school, Mrs. Buford. He's industrious; he'll make lots of money!" My mother hung her head in a moment of silence. That was the first time in my life that I realized some people say things without thinking. Mrs. Anderson, by default, had prescribed a prophecy of gloom to which my mother and I would have no part.

Fast forward…When I graduated from DePaul University with a degree in Curriculum Development, with a specialization in Economics Ed., with honors, I knew my view of leadership had changed for the better. All people will have a well-meaning yet misguided Mrs. Anderson appear in their lives from time to time. I never looked back on that situation, and neither should you, the reader, no matter what detractors toss in front of you. Again, great leaders are cultivated, not necessarily born. Always see obstacles in the school, business, community, or church as an opportunity for a "teachable" moment geared towards making the observer/participant a better leader.

An excellent example of leadership can be seen in the book of Exodus 18. Here, we are introduced to an outstanding business and leadership model through the story of Moses and his father-in-law, Jethro. Moses received sound advice from his father-in-law that all forward-thinking managers, administrators and business leaders ought to adopt and take to heart. As Solomon might say, there is truly nothing new under the sun.

As discussed earlier in the book of Exodus, from morning to evening, Moses would be engaged in settling disputes among the people. Daily, from early morning, the people would be standing around as they waited for Moses to hear their cases. Moses had not delegated any of the many cases he had at hand to anyone else. Jethro noticed this and was quick to point to Moses. He said, "What you are doing is not good. You and the people with you will certainly wear yourselves out, for the thing is too heavy for you."

Obviously, Jethro was wise to perceive that this behavior pattern would bring total exhaustion to Moses. What most readers of this passage from the Bible do not see is that his behavior would also negatively affect the people he served. The court stood at the risk of getting backlogged; the nation would likely become frustrated, and eventually, a possibility arose that many would give up on the idea of ever obtaining justice. Something needed to be done about Moses' leadership skills to prevent an adverse situation that was sure to arise.

The Good Intentions of Moses

Moses had the best interests at heart for his people. He desired that the people understand and appreciate the law. He took his responsibility and influence seriously. He judged each case as each mattered to him and more to God. Essentially, he was micro-managing things by channeling all the problems of his people to him, which posed more of a challenge in the long run.

Single-handedly, Moses was dealing with everything that confronted Israel. Jethro saw the possibility of him burning out and advised him to delegate some of the responsibilities to several trusted people. However, Moses would continue representing the nation before God, teaching the people godly principles and showing them what to do and how to live (Exodus 18:13–24).

Application Today

The unwillingness of leaders to delegate tasks to team members in either business or any other type of organization is very evident in today's society. However, there are possibilities of serious consequences if we allow the concept of our calling or sacred duty to turn into some form of micro-management. Take the example of the church, where 80% of the work is done by 20% of its members. A more in-depth look at business entities of today would yield similar results. It is incumbent upon the leaders of tomorrow to tap into this existing and rich professional climate to get the most productive output from a reluctant work base; not looking down the road expecting things to happen sometime in the future.

Whenever a leader becomes adamant about approving or making every decision, the outcome is an organizational bottleneck. Leaders need to understand that they can only accomplish so much before they get worn out and exhausted. However, instead of delegating the decision-making process, they tend to engineer the existing system to accommodate their limited time. This could work for some time, but it simply amounts to restructuring the whole organization around the leader's limitations in the long run. This is exactly the opposite of how effective leadership ought to work.

So, what lessons can be cultivated from the Jethro Model?

As a leader, you've got to promote a positive outlook and vision. Maybe, you've already pondered on the "why" aspect. Yes, you've understood or grasped the enormity of your special calling. Then, now you will want to mobilize a small team of strong people to assist you in figuring out the "how." However, you realize that a single person may not be sufficient to make your vision into a reality.

Now, this is where the challenge lies. To lead a good and able team, you first need to nurture and develop your own leadership potential. How, then, do you get to be an effective leader? The advice of Jethro on the need for effective organization and administration in the camp of Moses can be applied to improve any context of leadership, be it in your business, company/organization or even family. Some of the lessons of ef ficient leadership we get to know from Jethro's Model include:

1. Effective leaders go before God on behalf of the people.

It's important to plan on regular communion with God and to continually pray for direction, wisdom and ideas about your vision. You need to realize that you are in need of another source of strength that goes beyond the self. "Be anxious for nothing, but in everything by prayer and supplication with thanksgiving let your requests be made known to God." (Philippians 4:6)

2. Effective leaders understand their own limitations.

Progressive leadership is certainly not a one-person show. The burden of a truly inspiring and compelling vision is too big to be carried alone. When the single leader burns out, everything also burns out. There is a difference between wanting to lead and being talented to lead. When it comes to communication, one must always have someone, in addition to a spouse or other nuclear family members, affirm their ability to speak to people in a non-threatening way. One must perfect "people" skills in order to manage people effectively, be it volunteers or paid staff.

3. Effective leaders teach

I am reminded of a dreadful stain on the history of America. When the news of the death of one great leader, Dr. Martin

Luther King, was just new and a breaking story, Robert Kennedy, a leader at the time, handled it flawlessly. One extraordinary trait that Kennedy portrayed was how frank and calm he was when he addressed the hate and anger that underlie irrational acts. Much like the frustration felt by Black males when unscrupulous police practice brutality in the Urban Centers of America. Kennedy explained what had happened calmly. He showed no emotion and how the act had not angered him. His audience emulated his calm and collectiveness.

Kennedy had the ability to empathize with his listeners. One memorable moment in these speeches was when he was able to connect to his audience by reminding them that his own brother was also killed—"by a white man." The implicit in this is aberrant—the peculiar habit of stereotyping, whether about religion, race, or any other widespread, sweeping belief/ideas/options. He pushed for a deeper understanding. Then, he referenced some words that helped him. Kennedy said: My favorite poet, **_Aeschylus,_** once wrote, "And even in our sleep, pain which cannot forget falls drop by drop upon the heart, until in our own despair, against our will, comes wisdom through the awful grace of God."

As a leader, you must develop a passion for mentoring, engaging and teaching other leaders. In management, the real leadership test is your ability to reproduce yourself in others. Inspire the team you assemble to buy into your vision until they become part of it and also want to own it as much as you do.

The 3 **T**'s outlined by the Jethro Model for effective management of people:

Teach—instruct those entrusted to your care with simple, easy steps.

Tell—verbally exemplify by way of illustration, but don't procrastinate!

Train—give yourself (body language) as a tangible example and follow-up.

4. Effective leaders develop and create strong teams.

The most efficient and effective way of creating a strong team is to make a list of qualities you wish to see among your candidates and base your selections on this criterion. With your selected and committed team, share your vision, which, in turn, they will teach to others.

5. Effective leaders delegate

Great leaders focus on the larger macro picture and then break it down into smaller chunks that are manageable. These small tasks are then assigned to trusted team members.

6. Effective leaders develop an accountability system.

A good accountability system will not only increase one's performance and success but will also keep you engaged and validate your thoughts and ideas. This is also a biblically based principle. Jesus Himself demanded from the Disciples an account of what they had taught or done. "And the apostles gathered themselves together unto Jesus and told him all things, both what they had done, and what they had taught." (Mark 6:30)

7. Effective leaders empower and encourage excellence.

An effective leader will encourage dedication and commitment by assisting his team to become organized, even in their family and personal lives. Also, he will take part in stimulating their personal and professional development.

What the Bible, through Jethro and Moses, Teaches us About Leadership and Delegation

After 400 years of living in slavery, Moses had just begun leading the Israelites out of Egypt. His task was to take the children of God to Israel, their promised land. As we read in the Book of Exodus Chapter 18, Moses was laboring in the middle of the Sinai desert from dawn to very late into the night as he attempted to resolve the countless conflicts that were coming up among the Children of Israel. Effectively, Moses had unintentionally turned into a workaholic.

Jethro, his father-in-law, a Midian priest, saw that the workload Moses was putting upon himself could not be sustained for long and that he was heading for troubled times ahead. Wisely, he pulled Moses aside and, after commending him for his efforts at doing God's bidding (Exodus 18:9–12), gave him a couple of priceless lessons and counsel regarding the benefits of delegation.

In today's business world, Jethro articulated several management principles that were relevant to the situation of Moses then and which can be applied even today.

Admit to yourself that non-stop working is unsustainable

Jethro didn't hold anything back! In a matter-of-fact manner, he told Moses that what he was doing was certainly not good. It was neither good for Moses nor for the people Moses was leading, as both stood at the risk of wearing themselves out. He explained to Moses how what he was doing was too much for one person to perform all by himself.

Effectively, Jethro was telling Moses that, eventually, he would break down. Does that ring a warning bell in you? We all know that you can't keep working 12-hour days, six days a week, and still expect to come out unscathed. Eventually, something will give way: Either your sanity, your health, your career, your family, or your own promising legacy. Even worse, Moses stood at the risk of wearing out his people. For your sake—and that of your people, you must appreciate and admit the reality. Your current strategy is not working.

Know that yours is a unique calling.

Jethro had seen something extremely significant. He saw that while Moses perhaps could do lots of things quite well, he appeared to have a unique calling in which he alone brought more value. As we see in Chapter 18, verses 19-20 of the Book of Exodus, Jethro exhorted Moses: "Listen now to my voice; I will give you counsel, and God will be with you: Stand before God for the people, so that you may bring the difficulties to God. And you shall teach them the statutes and the laws and show them the way in which they must walk and the work they must do."

Precisely what Jethro, his own father-in-law, was telling him was that he needed to offload himself of those things that other people could perform so that he could give his attention to those things that only he could perform or do, namely going before God and teaching the people what to do.

This is a principle that applies to you as a leader. In whatever you are doing, where exactly is it that you bring the most value—that special thing that you are personally, uniquely qualified and called to do? Then how can you go about delegating the rest?

Here, Jethro gets very practical and gently gives Moses a rebuke and warning, telling him he is not the only person who could get the job done. He needed to get some trusted leaders to help in sharing the load, as there was no reason why he should bear it alone. We see Jethro in verse 21 telling Moses: "Moreover you shall select from all the people able men, such as fear God, men of truth, [and] hating covetousness....."

Worth noting here is that Jethro's focus is on their character. Your chosen people can gain experience and the necessary knowledge, they can master skills and even greatly develop their personal leadership gifts, but the place where you must begin is with a solid foundation of a godly character. With such a character, it becomes much easier for you to delegate effectively and with confidence.

Give your chosen leaders real authority and responsibility.

Jethro was apparently a very practical man. He clearly understood that a typical leader's span of control is around ten people. He guided Moses in setting up a simplified organizational hierarchy that had different responsibility levels. He gave a clear outline: "... and place such over them to be rulers of thousands, rulers of hundreds, rulers of fifties, and rulers of tens. And let them judge the people at all times" (Ex. 18: 21b).

This is certainly not complex rocket science, and neither is it a bureaucratic setup. The various levels of management proposed by Jethro were not designed to hamper or impede the decision-making process but rather to facilitate it and make it more effective. The key lies in giving your chosen leaders real authority. Yes, they are bound to make mistakes, but you must get over that. This is the price that comes with developing leaders.

Only undertake what others can't

Jethro advised Moses to manage by exception: "And let them judge the people at all seasons: and it shall be, that every great matter they shall bring unto thee, but every small matter they shall judge: so shall it be easier for thyself, and they shall bear the burden with thee." (Ex18:22b)

The Navigators founder, Dawson Trotman, once observed that a leader should never do anything of great significance that other people in the team can do or will do when so much of important things to be done are there that others cannot do by themselves or are not going to do. This is definitely an invaluable piece of advice for every good leader. Identify where you can bring unique added value, let that be your main focus and let everything else go.

How does Jethro conclude his counsel to Moses?

"If you do this thing, and God so commands you, then you will be able to endure, and all these people will also go to their places in peace."(Ex 18:23)

It is important to note how the experienced priest Jethro promises Moses two beneficial possible outcomes:

1. Moses himself will endure (Strategy Sustainability)
2. People will have peace (Fewer Conflicts).

When in doubt...delegate!

The advice of Jethro to Moses wasn't about streamlining the court. Neither was it about appointing people to summarize for him the information so he could dispense faster verdicts. Rather, the wise counsel of Jethro was to delegate: to mentor and train other upcoming leaders who could assume some aspects of the authority of Moses and be part of taking care of the nation. Moses would then become a leader rather than the one holding back everybody. He could now handle his portion of the workload, and the people wouldn't get necessarily frustrated. Upcoming leaders would get trained for bigger things, and people would get justice administered faster.

By following the above principles, you start bearing the burden of your bigger vision with some other like-minded persons. This way, you will be serving alongside dedicated and happy people who will be helping you to avoid burning out, endure the journey, and finally finish well—the great rewards that come with effective leadership.

Management ability is not an inborn characteristic but is something that is learned. Good leaders are made and not born. God called Moses to lead the children of Israel, yet even with many years of education acquired in Egypt plus the practical experience, he still had a lot to learn. This ought to be an encouraging thing to those who feel that perhaps administration is not their forte. We can learn from the case of Moses and Jethro that it's possible to learn how to become better administrators, better managers, and ultimately better leaders.

One of the key principles we also learn from this story is the influence principle of leadership. For Moses to lead the Israelites, he had to influence the masses. A leader in today's society needs to have true influence over the people they are leading.

We also learn that leadership is a process. Moses, as a leader, was evolving. We can see from the time God first came to him and to the phase of his settling conflicts that he had grown more as a leader, becoming better along the way. The traits of true leadership are not developed over night but through hard work and learning over time.

The empowerment principle of leadership is also important. A key factor in empowering others is a high belief in your people or team. Only secure leaders give power to others. For Moses to delegate some of his responsibilities to others, he had to share his knowledge with them. A true leader is able to share the know-how and his skills to get the work done. This includes leading by lifting others to a degree of selflessness. Only secure leaders can give themselves away like Moses.

For a leader to accomplish a task, he needs to prioritize. A good leader will need to answer these questions.

1. What is required?
2. What gives the greatest return?

3. What brings the greatest reward?

Additionally, timing is key to efficient leadership. Great leaders recognize that *when* to lead is as important as *what* to do and *where* to go. When the right leader and the right timing come

together, incredible things happen. Jethro's timing was perfect because if Moses had continued with his way, chaos would have started.

Finally, we all need to understand that Leadership is a skill that can be learned. Therefore, leadership is proactive – problem-solving, looking ahead, and not being satisfied with the status quo or being complacent. Everybody won't always agree, even when the outcome is proven effective.

Many years ago, while cable channel surfing, I stumbled upon a Christian station and heard Dr. Robert H. Schuller, one of the most successful preachers in the world at the time (The Crystal Cathedral), discuss the harmful effects of what he called the "80/20 rule" (see chapter 6 for further clarity). He then gave his definition of this occurrence in the church but also related how it is true in most segments of society and our families in general: Twenty percent of the people do 80% of the work while most of the rest do little or nothing. Consequently, he interconnected various strategies by which a church's leadership might begin to address the issues of member mobilization and development. Again, the 80/20 rule is not a church only issue; this endeavor must be cultivated by all of those who are leaders or expressing an interest in getting a job done in the public or private sector as managers of people. Everyone will not agree on the pastor/leader's course of action.

As a spearhead, you will have many opportunities to make decisions that someone with an alternative motive or private agenda will subsequently challenge. Don't be discouraged when you run into one of the 80 percenters...be brave; God will always sustain you in the end, so hang in there!

10 Character Traits of a Successful Leader:

A good leader must reveal their passion regarding their objectives and vision. They are straightforward and a good manager of resources. They articulate expectations and ideas that are not only genuine and satisfying but also assist their team to improve by being open, sincere, and objective.

A good leader is an innate hard worker with a full understanding of core business ideas. They have a strong eye for specifics, accountability and time management, encouraging discipline and focus among the members of the team. They are firm yet fair and open-minded when making choices. A good leader is forward-thinking, structured and thoughtful, always preserving the big picture as the main goal. They have both long-term and short-term goals that drive the daily objectives of the team.

Individuals and their teams grow when a leader leads by example. A well-thought-of leader has the aptitude to delegate and entrust tasks to others, making room for growth and permitting the leader to spend time efficiently. The following is a list of what should be a blueprint for operational leaders in any organization, public or private. Conviction is significant for a leader. The leader should always be thinking about the subsequent opportunities, the next generation, and the next leader. The leader must carry out decisions that will benefit people, both in the short-term but also in the future. Also, they ought to create and carry out a long-term plan to lead to accomplishment. Most importantly, a great leader needs to generate new leaders. Complete a self-reflection and see if you have the required qualities for effective leadership.

1. **Honesty:** A typical leadership quality that speaks to a leader's credibility. Those who are honest, particularly about apprehensions, make it possible that complications, once they present themselves, are going to be addressed instead of avoided. Honesty permits better growth and improvement within any organizational structure.

2. **Compassion:** Generating a legitimate understanding of your staff will make it more difficult for resentment and personal issues to creep in and upset group efforts. Suppose your crew is aware that you are compassionate relative to their concerns. In that case, they'll be more than happy to work with you and be a part of your vision rather than foster undesirable feelings and participate in counter-organizational activities.

3. **Communication:** Operational communication helps to keep the team functioning and focused on the right assignments and also fosters a sense of positive approach. If you talk effectively about instruction, issues and expectations, your workforce will be more inclined to respond and meet your objectives.

4. **Direction:** Having the ambition to break out of the standard and aim for extraordinary effects, as well as the means to achieve those goals, is an indispensable characteristic of a good leader. By early detection of what may be lurking down the road, good foresight, and managing goals through the objectives, a good leader can generate remarkable change for the better.

5. **Flexibility:** Not every problem demands the same solution. Being flexible to ideas and being open-minded about them increases the chance that you'll find the best answer possible. Flexibility will also set a respectable

example for your team and foster a system that rewards innovative ideas in the process.

6. **Vision:** Humbly put, know where you're headed. Picture it within your head, and talk about it efficiently. This isn't just the idea of having the foresight to look to the future as an ordinary pastor, principal, manager or CEO. It is critically significant that you are capable of painting a glowing picture of where your organization or group is headed. In the end, use this dream to guide and motivate action, as well as sharing your vision with your group. All members of your group ought to be able to designate a similar image and communicate it effectively without fear of retribution.

7. **Conviction:** A strong dream and the inclination to see it achieved, is one of the important natures of management. The leader who has faith in the mission and works towards it will be a motivational plus and serve as a valuable resource to their supporters in spite of their personal beliefs or feelings as it relates to the end result.

8. **Engagement**: Be thorough when dealing with internal conflict. A keystone of working professionally with individuals is being secure in dealing with this battle. The common sense is that conflict will be inevitable in any working environment. There is no surprise there; people will have different ideas about how to achieve the same result, and those will inevitably result in disagreements. Learn how to efficiently resolve encounters and harness the optimum production from the people you manage.

9. **Trust**: Be a reliable leader. People want to accomplish their goals and follow those who are projecting great viewpoints and forward-thinking ideas. All things being equal, a trustworthy leader is going to get much more

from his people and have a much more robust following. Be somebody your people can have faith in. It is significant to remember that it takes time to trust someone; trust comes with time. The reverse is that you can stop trusting someone quickly. Don't be a casualty of your own war!

10. **Consistency:** Being a dependable leader will gain you credibility and respect, which is vital in receiving a buy-in from the association or group you represent. By setting a standard of credibility and fairness, your crew will want to perform similarly. It's not about self-promotion. It's about serving others. It's about teaching others. It's about helping others achieve their potential each person...every time. It's about the mission.

Remember that strong leaders uphold consistent and clear communication with their personnel. Constant, effective communication helps an association's members understand that the establishment's mission and vision are unique and gives them a declaration that they're working towards the sought-after goals. Communication is always vital because it's so significant in instituting work expectancies, giving productive responses and cross-training new bodies for alternate work accessibility. All these qualities are found in the humbleness of a personality that leads by an optimistic example, one that says: "Treat the general public the way you want to be treated." As will be discussed consistently in this book, leaders are rarely, if ever, born- they are cultivated. Do you think you have what it takes? *Teaching, Telling, and Training are* vital in the process of creating great leaders; they are major components in the developmental process of any trailblazer, so if your goal is to become a leader, work on developing these characteristics with a view to your own limitations. If you feel you are not cut-out for leadership and its distinctions, then at least be willing to support the process in your school, church, community, corporation etc., contributing by way of active participation as a "team player". Now go out there and have some fun collaborating...and don't forget to smile as if God were watching you!

CHAPTER 2
Effective Leaders Don't Procrastinate!

Tell

If you wait for perfect conditions, you'll never get anything done.

He that observeth the wind shall not sow; he that regardeth the clouds shall not reap. *(Ecclesiastes 11:4)*. Telling the truth is critical for leaders of today, as it was true in Moses' day: "Never put off tomorrow what is **due** today." This became clear as I was completing the research for my decision-making book, **You Can Stop Procrastination Today!** Although it is written from a Christian perspective, the tenets are applicable to people from all backgrounds, Christian or otherwise. Moses had a good idea yet allowed Jethro to point out areas for improvement, which included procrastination.

There are many possible definitions of procrastination, but, in essence, procrastination is the practice of doing less urgent or unimportant tasks instead of more urgent ones or doing more pleasurable activities instead of less pleasurable ones. Procrastinators put off impending tasks until a later time, sometimes to the "last minute" before the deadline. To some extent, everyone procrastinates. Unfortunately, when chronic procrastination becomes a habit, it can become damaging to one's life. People often procrastinate because they experience more short-term pleasure from the less urgent tasks.

More often than not, we pray fervently to God for something we want without attempting to work towards that which we desire. How do we know if God has answered our prayer without actually working towards our goal? It is important to understand that God does not work in magical ways but in miraculous ways. Faith without obedience is dead. Prayer without action is wasted. What would your life look like if you stopped praying for God's will and just did what you wanted instead? How would your church look if you spent as much time serving as it spent praying about serving?

The truth is, sometimes, when you think you're praying, you're really just procrastinating; when you think you're asking for God's will to be done, you're really just telling Him "no." In times that demand action, prayer can be disobedience in disguise. Wasted prayer uncovers the ways we use prayer to dodge responsibility for the work God has assigned to us. In this writer's opinion, religion has eaten some people raw. Most people don't know God, even if they fervently claim to. They don't know the principles that guide the universe, and they misunderstand the teachings of God. It is written that "faith without work is useless." This saying was not made by man but by God.

Put another way, you procrastinate when you put off things that you should be focusing on right now, usually in favor of doing something that is more enjoyable or that makes you more comfortable. We are more comfortable doing things that are pleasurable instead of those that are of paramount importance to us. Such action reminds us of the old saying, "you can't have your cake and eat it too." If you must do those things that you are excited about, and let's say you desire something very important, you are indirectly forgoing your wish or desire. Procrastinators never get anything done. They are always looking for the right time or the right mood before they can start to work. Unfortunately, the perfect time to do something will never appear. Now is always the best time to do something. The only way to complete your goals is to begin.

There are many notable quotes made by distinguished people that will stop you from procrastinating. Still, I prefer this quote from Abraham Lincoln: "You cannot escape the responsibility of tomorrow by evading it today." The world is getting more advanced, and things are getting easier day-by-day as a result of the ideas and work of men who didn't procrastinate but rather worked diligently towards achieving their goals and never stopped until they achieved them. Charles Dickens wrote another lovely quote on procrastination: "Procrastination is the thief of time; collar him."

There is the same 24-hour day for everyone. Your success rate is proportional to or dependent on how wisely you use your time. Those who are happy now were not intimidated by new projects. They got started. They never delayed because they understood that important tasks have scary appearances. They also understood that the work would never be completed if they didn't take action. "You may delay, but time will not," Benjamin Franklin correctly stated.

Biblical-Based Steps to Overcoming Procrastination

Imagine what your local church assembly would be like if everyone spent as much time serving others as they did praying about serving others. Usually, when you may think you are praying, you could, in fact, just be procrastinating.

When you are telling God that His Will be done, you could be disobeying Him, despite your best intentions. Wasted prayer exposes the manner in which we utilize prayer to evade responsibility for the duty and work assigned to us by God. You may need to get off your knees and begin to live like a true and genuine Christian instead of simply praying like one. The time to stop praying and begin doing has arrived, and it's today!

1. "The craving of a sluggard [procrastinator] will be the death of him because his hands refuse to work" (Proverbs 21:25). Acknowledge and admit that procrastination is smothering all of your inspiration.
2. "There is a proper time and procedure for every matter ..." (Ecclesiastes 8:6a). Honestly, tell God that you're tired of struggling with the clock and start praying for help and wisdom to use the time assigned to you by God.
3. "..... there will be a time for every activity, a time to judge every deed" (Ecclesiastes 3:17b). Keep a record of everything you need to do in a planner and check off the tasks as you accomplish them.
4. "... he who follows empty pursuits will have poverty in plenty" (Proverbs 28:19b). Refuse to be distracted from your major goals by minor, less important ones

by keeping your focus on the main thing through effective prioritizing of each day's tasks.

5. "Suppose one of you wants to build a tower. Won't you first sit down and estimate the cost to see if you have enough money to complete it? For if you lay the foundation and are not able to finish it, everyone who sees it will ridicule you" (Luke 14:28–29). Carefully assess the time required to successfully finish each task realistically, with extra time allotted for unexpected delays.

6. "Do not throw away your confidence; it will be richly rewarded. You need to persevere so that when you have done the will of God, you will receive what he has promised" (Hebrews 10:35–36). Strongly resist the temptation of feeling guilty whenever unforeseen situations come up to hinder you from accomplishing the day's tasks. Re-plan tomorrow's activities, but don't forget about the missed work today!

7. "May these words of my mouth and the meditation of my heart be pleasing in your sight, LORD, my Rock and my Redeemer" (Psalm 19:14 NIV 2011). Recognize and root out any negative self-talk that dares to intrude on your thoughts and your self-dialogue. Try to be reflective of God's truth and love for you.

8. "The way of a fool *is* right in his own eyes: but he that hearkeneth unto counsel *is* wise" (Proverbs 12:15). Ask a trusted friend or fellow worshipper to assist whenever you struggle, especially at the beginning.

9. "I have been crucified with Christ, and I no longer live, but Christ lives in me; and the life which I now live in the flesh I live by the faith of the Son of God,

who loved me, and gave himself for me" (Galatians 2:20). Yield your whole life to Jesus Christ, giving Him total and full control.

10. "His divine power has given us everything we need for a Godly life through our knowledge of Him who called us by his own glory and goodness. Through these, he has given us his very great and precious promises, so that through them you may participate in the divine nature, having escaped the corruption in the world caused by evil desires" (2 Peter 1:3–4). Go ahead and rightfully claim what God has promised. Philippians 4:13 (NKJV) **I can do all things through Christ who strengthens me.**

Prioritizing Task

It is important for us to know and understand the causes of procrastination because only then can we produce a solution. One of the major causes of procrastination is fear. Many people are afraid to do something that involves a lot of energy. Another cause of procrastination is laziness. Laziness is the mother of procrastination. Lazy people can hardly complete any task. Disorganization can also cause procrastination. So many people spend their precious time doing what they don't need to do or working on their least important task. We must solve the problem of procrastination by overcoming our fears, engaging ourselves in useful activities and finally arranging our work in order of importance. If we work on the most important task first and follow a strict schedule, procrastination will be a mere distant memory.

CHAPTER 3
Body Language and Leadership

Train

Body language was applied by Bible characters even before the King James Version of the Bible came into existence. Body language is older and more innate in humans than even spoken or facial language. All Church and Business leaders should know and practice these principles as Moses did. Consider this: People born blind can perform the same body language expressions as people who can see. These body language expressions come pre-programmed within our brains. I've always been incredibly fascinated with body language and how it helps us achieve our goals in life. Our nonverbal communications govern how other people think and feel about us.

If you are anything like this writer, then you've had a healthy obsession with body language for some time. In recent years, a few fascinating studies at Harvard, Princeton and other top universities have shed new light on body language and how to use it at work or other social interactions. Although the power of language is extremely important in conveying the right message, the power of body language, however, might be the determining factor of how someone makes us feel. Here is an insight into some of the latest studies on how we can use body language to our advantage in everyday life. **Your body expresses emotion better than your face:** We all grow up learning how to deal with each other based on facial expressions. But that might not be the most effective way to judge other people's emotions. You can ask any number of people to judge from photography whether people are experiencing joy, loss, victory or pain. Try it yourself; it actually works!

Now, it gets even more interesting. Body language isn't just something we have to learn. Most emotional expressions come built into our system. For example, scientists from British Columbia observed congenitally blind people at the Paralympics. In a vibrant example, some athletes can see, as compared to those congenitally blind. Yet, after winning, both express the same body language for victory: So, if body language is both so ancient and ingrained, so powerful in expressing our true emotions, how can we use it better in our everyday lives to achieve what we want?

Body language changes who you are – literally:

In one of my favorite Ted Talks (TED. 2007), Amy Cuddy explains some of the most peculiar happenings of body language. Cuddy focuses a lot on the business world and how body language is helpful to us in this area, and the possibilities seem endless. Cuddy distinguishes between 2 different types of body postures. Some are powerful poses, others less so. She argues that expressing more powerful poses helps us get better jobs, makes us feel better and makes us more successful overall. And yet, it goes a lot further than just changing the position of your legs or arms. Cuddy explains that, inside our bodies, actual changes happen as our body language changes. These changes largely have to do with hormones.

The two hormones in question are:

- **Testosterone**: The "power" hormone, which, amongst lots of other things, helps us be better leaders, stay more focused and be more attentive.
- **Cortisol**: The "stress" hormone, which makes us less reactive to stress, easily overwhelmed and powerless.

Here is what Cuddy's experiment contained: They brought people into a room. For two minutes, they would either perform a powerful pose or a powerless pose. Then, they would go on to perform a job interview. The results were absolutely stunning: Neutral recruiters, who didn't know who performed which pose, consistently picked only those who had performed the powerful poses as people they would want to hire. On top of that, the actual hormone levels of the people involved changed dramatically. There was a marked increase in testosterone levels and a drop in cortisol after performing the power-pose (for just 2 minutes!). Changing our body language doesn't just change our outcomes. It changes who we are as people. So instead of "faking it until you make it," my advice is 'fake it until you become it.' Can you fake it until you make it? Yes, here are 5 postures to work on today to answer the question, **"How can I improve my body language?"**

How to improve your body language – Here are 5 postures to work on

1. Focus on the position of your feet

Kinsey Goman has researched the importance of body language in the workplace for many years. One of her best tips is to watch your feet (Goman et al. 2008). A lot of the time, we focus on our upper body or faces, yet our feet reveal more about our emotions than we might think. When you approach 2 people talking, you will be acknowledged in one of two ways; if the feet of your two colleagues stay in place and they twist only their upper torsos in your direction, they don't really want you to join the conversation. But if their feet are open to include you, then you know that you are truly invited to participate.

2. Smile – it'll make you happier.

We smile because we are happy. But does it work the other way around, too? Researchers at Cardiff University think so. Michael Lewis, a co-author of the study, says that people who smile without actually feeling happy can make themselves feel a lot happier. It would appear that the way we experience emotions isn't just restricted to our brain—there are parts of our bodies that help and reinforce the feelings we're having. Of course, being able to smile fully is another story. But for now, give it a try to smile in the restroom or another quiet place before a difficult conversation, job interview, or meeting. It might just make you more successful.

3. Practice the "Superman" stance prior to important meetings/interviews.

As stated earlier, studies have shown that 'posing' (such as the "Superman" stance) is an ideal form of body language to use before a job interview, as it can help boost confidence. Suppose you're nervous about going in for an interview. In that case, research has shown that posing—for example, standing in a manner to suggest confidence for a few minutes can make you feel more confident during the interview or meeting. It makes you feel like a superhero (ta dahhh!!!) like you can take on the world. Try this one prior to an interview in a quiet place and see if it has the same results for you.

4. Realign your body more congenially with your conversation partner.

Another great tip from Goman states that if you try to align yourself more congenially with your conversation partner, you will be able to solve tension in conversations and come to solutions more quickly. I've found this especially true when meeting people for the first time (Goman et al. 2008). It's usually hard to build rapport at first, so focusing on aligning your body favorably can make a big difference. Give it a try.

5. Lower your voice with deep, even breathing.

Though not a specific tip for physical body posture, this is one of my favorites. Men and women with deeper voices are more likely to land in leadership positions and are generally perceived as a greater authority. To lower your voice, especially before an interview, try to take some deep belly breaths. It will relax your throat area, which generally contracts and raises the pitch of your voice.

Background on Hand Gestures as a Form of Body Language

(Beware of the Handshake: It Hides a Snake!)

People from all walks of life must always realize that handshakes have been practiced since at least the 2nd century B.C. Moses himself would have engaged in this practice. Many researchers believe that the handshake originated in the Western world. It was a gesture of peace, demonstrated by the fact that the hands held no weapons.

Today, a handshake is offered upon meeting or parting. It is an expression of goodwill, gratitude, and congratulations. Many people believe that a handshake reveals something about the character of the person who gives it. A firm handshake reflects a confident personality, while a floppy handshake reveals a shy one. A handshake is a clasping usually of right hands by two people (as in greeting or farewell) as defined in the online Merriam-Webster dictionary. Handshakes are an important introductory ritual within social interactions, and research has demonstrated that the quality of the handshake does impact an individual's impression of another. In general, a firm handshake implies power, strength, and intelligence, while a weak handshake implies weakness, uncertainty, and apathy. As we will discuss further in this chapter, the antiquity of the handshake is thought to be related to an assessment of aggression. Showing and gripping hands would show that no weapons were concealed and no harm was meant towards the other.

Recent scientific research reveals that chemicals such as oxytocin related to harmony and friendship are released in the brain when touching occurs. Negative emotions sensed during a handshake are important as they contribute to the impression of the other individual. These negative emotions are stored in the fight-or-flight area brain as a warning to avoid anything that threatens us.

There are varied cultural versions and meanings of the handshake. Similar gestural meanings can vary from one culture to another. No reference will be made to the "middle finger salute" known around the globe as a gesture of ill will. Worldwide, the handshake is done with the right hand. It is considered rude or insulting to offer a handshake with your left hand in cultures where the left hand is used for personal hygiene. Gender can also influence handshaking. In Western culture, handshaking has become expected of women since joining the workforce in the 20th century. Some cultures do not allow women to touch others, so there is a different demonstration of greeting.

The strength demonstrated during a handshake will vary from one culture to another. Firm handshakes are desired in Western culture as weak handshakes infer weakness of character. In contrast, weak handshakes are expected in China, although there is a longer holding of hands. A too-firm handshake in some Muslim countries is considered rude. Sub-cultures such as secret societies and sports teams, in addition to geographical regions and cultures, can dictate the method of a handshake. This sub-culture specificity includes types of evolved handshakes such as thumb-turns, fist-bumping and high-fiving. Good leaders/managers know how to implement and how to interpret a specific handshake.

Types of Handshakes

Several documented styles of handshake have come to infer certain feelings and meanings. **The Pusher** shakes your hand but extends his arm so that you can't get too close. He needs physical and emotional space, which must be respected if you want to be his friend. **The Puller** manipulates you by leading you with his arm, often unbeknownst to you. ***The Two-Handed Handshake***, with the left hand wrapping over the right hand in contact, is thought to be the warmest. Political studies show that it is sincere if the left-hand stays on your hand, but if the hand moves up the arm or to the elbow, they are trying to get something from you. The Top-Hand holds his hand horizontally so that his hand is on top of yours, signifying dominance and superiority.

In contrast, if the hand is held horizontally beneath yours (bottom-handed), they consider themselves inferior. ***The Twister*** starts as a regular handshake but then their hand ends up on top of yours in a gesture of superiority. ***The Crusher*** performs a basic handshake but squeezes too hard; his enthusiasm has gotten in the way.

The Finger Squeeze, Polite Pinch, and Dead Fish are types of handshakes where the palms do not touch, only the finger, creating a superficial greeting. These types are thought to be related to low self-esteem, a desire to hide their true feelings, a fear of connecting, apathy, or nervousness about the encounter. These types of handshakes evoke negative emotions since the physical connection is impaired.

Studies have shown that people form impressions based on the quality of the handshake, which reflects a part of their personality. However, it can become a developed skill with good practice and the intent to evoke the emotions you desire in business or healthy relationships. According to Mark Perl (Linked In. 2014), there are 10 things one should know in order to master the art of handshaking:

Ten Tips for Giving a Handshake

1. Your grip should be firm but not bone-crushing (consider age and gender)

2. Maintain eye contact (however brief the handshake maybe). It conveys confidence and openness. For most people, if another fails to make eye contact, the word 'shifty' immediately comes to mind (not good for your branding!)

3. Always accompany a handshake with a welcoming smile.

4. Give deliberate and controlled oscillation (handshakes up and down) from the elbow. Two or three pumps suffice. Too much shaking can convey over-excitement and, in some cases, may give the impression that you are desperate.

5. Lean in. Forward body positioning conveys commitment

6. Let it last about three seconds

7. Release the other's hand, even if the verbal introduction continues

8. Use the other person's name in conjunction with the handshake. This clearly indicates to the other person that you feel they are important to you (as you have made an effort to remember their name from their introduction) and that you value them. Combining the use of their name and the handshake links you to them physically, verbally and, importantly, on an emotional level, too

9. Face the other person squarely. Failure to do so may indicate that you are not being 'straight' with your opposite, that you want to get away, that you feel the need to protect yourself or may indicate your

unwillingness to engage fully or connect during the interaction.

10. Rise if seated. Failure to do so conveys an unmistakable message of indifference.

CHAPTER 4
The Stress Factor

STRESS SHOULD NEVER GET THE BEST OF CHRISTIANS

As Moses is leading the people of Israel from Egypt, where they escaped captivity to the Promised Land, He learns a valuable lesson from Jethro that helps Moses become a better leader throughout the wilderness days of Israel's journey. The instruction that Jethro gives to Moses will also serve us well in teaching us how to handle the stress that creeps, and sometimes floods, into our lives.

In Exodus 18, Jethro comes to visit Moses in the wilderness and brings back Moses' wife and family that Moses had sent to him for safe keeping. When Jethro arrives, he greets Moses with great words of encouragement about all that he had heard Moses was doing in leading the nation of Israel. The next day, Moses convened the court to make all the judgments about disputes that people had. When Jethro saw all that Moses was doing, Jethro warned Moses that if he kept up that pace of responsibility, he would burn out and not be able to help anyone. The stress was too great for Moses. Jethro gave Moses some suggestions on how to handle the situation better to lessen the weight and relieve some of the stress. Here are the **3 T** concepts (Teach,

Tell and Train) to learn from Jethro and Moses about how to handle stress:

TEACH: TRUST GOD TO DO HIS PART.

First, Jethro encouraged Moses to take the disputes and the decisions to the Lord. Jethro gave this instruction:

Listen now to me and I will give you some advice, and may God be with you. You must be the people's representative before God and bring their disputes to him (Exodus 18:19, NIV).

Jethro was advising Moses to let God decide. Let God carry the weight of the tough decisions that Moses faced. God was wise enough to know exactly what to do. Rather than having to do it all himself, Moses should be letting the Lord direct the decisions and listening to what the right decision would be. This would take the pressure off Moses. He should rely more on God. When we get stressed, too often, we are stressed because we are depending too much on ourselves and too little on God. If you want to relieve stress in your life, trust God to do His part and walk in obedience to what He calls you to do. Let God handle it, and you just do what He says.

TELL: POUR INTO OTHERS SO THEY CAN GROW.

Another principle that Jethro communicated to Moses when he visited in the wilderness was for Moses to impart unto others how to do what needed to be done so they could do a better job of doing what was right and fewer issues would make it to Moses for him to decide. Jethro told Moses:

Teach them his decrees and instructions, and show them the way they are to live and how they are to behave (Exodus 18:20, NIV).

If the Israelites learned more of what God wanted from them and learned how to live those things out, there would be much fewer disputes for Moses to hear because people would be treating each other fairly.

When others around you grow, they can do more things correctly, which means you must do less. As others grow, your stress level decreases. Growing others takes time and effort, but the result is well worth it as your stress goes down.

TRAIN: INCLUDE OTHERS SO YOU DO NOT HAVE TO CARRY THE ENTIRE LOAD.

Finally, Jethro encouraged Moses to let others bear the responsibility for some of what Moses was carrying.

But select capable men from all the people – men who fear God, trustworthy men who hate dishonest gain – and appoint them as officials... (Exodus 18:21, NIV).

Rather than Moses deciding everything, Jethro told Moses to appoint others with different levels of responsibility to handle the easier decisions. Then, Moses would be freed up to hear the difficult cases and take those to the Lord.

When we allow others to share the load with us, we are carrying less of the load. This will greatly decrease our stress because we will no longer have to do it all, and we will have others to share in the journey.

Moses was stressed. Jethro gave Moses some pointers on how to set up for success and relieve some of the stress. We can learn how to lessen our stress as well. Trust God. Grow others. Let others help. The task will be done in a better way. And we will have less stress, too. That is a win-win.

The Moses Principle of Leadership: 10 Ways Christians Can Eliminate Stress

"It is better to set a hundred men to work than to do the work of a hundred men." (D.L. Moody)

1. Don't forget to pray!
2. Get proper sleep.
3. Rise and shine at the proper time.
4. Things that don't fit into the schedule may adversely affect one's mental/physical well-being.
5. Remember the advice of Moses' father-in-law: Delegate tasks to talented people.
6. Modernize and unblock your life.
7. Never put off tomorrow what is "*due*" today!
8. Permit proper time to get from point 'A" to point "B."
9. Never "bite off" more than you can chew!
10. Go slow.... Because... haste makes waste.

CHAPTER 5

Wartime vs. Peacetime Management Styles

Know When to Adjust!

As discussed throughout this book, every leader as far back as Moses, whether in business, politics, or the contemporary church, has what one might call a default style of leadership. In business, most of the time you're likely to be most effective and most comfortable when you are leading using *that* chosen default leadership style. However, the ability to adapt or mold your style of leadership is critical when you are required to deliver timely results on a regular basis while still presenting positive outcomes to receivers or followers. You'll never be an effective leader if you only practice as a crisis manager, one who only adjusts to problem situations as they arise. Instead, plan ahead!

Among the simplest and most powerful frameworks that can be of great assistance to you is to adapt the time-tested concept of peacetime and wartime leadership. The best thing about this leadership philosophy is that it's completely natural. Once you have grasped the difference between these two management or leadership roles, the framework you implement will continue to be very useful whenever you are thinking about the qualities of great leadership styles.

Peacetime Leadership

Peacetime in a business environment is when your company has a sustainable and clear-cut competitive advantage over your competitors. Your market is experiencing unprecedented growth, and you possess the skills, resources, and time to focus on innovation and market-based expansion. Because of these factors, you're likely to be focusing all your efforts on inclusive decision-making. Put in layman's terms: asking supporters for input on maintaining the status quo.

Leaders in peacetime broaden and maximize the current opportunity. A CEO during peacetime focuses on the big picture, empowering followers to make well-thought-out and detailed decisions. The goals of a peacetime CEO, manager or leader are big, daunting, awesome, and audacious. This type of manager is a visionary always looking to an optimistic future. A good peacetime manager always knows: ***"When outgo exceeds your income, upkeep becomes your downfall!"***

Wartime Leadership

Wartime, in a nutshell, may be described as the period when your business, organization, company or church is focused on a threat to its very survival. You typically have just a single remaining arrow in your quiver, and at all costs, it must hit the target. Survival depends upon strict alignment and adherence to this single survival mission. People don't always respond kindly to a new leader, even when that individual has essentially the same style. That's because people will oftentimes respond to a person more than the movement or challenges that lie ahead. Know when to adjust your management style for the better based on your followers.

Maximizing on Both Styles

The moment you start noticing that your company, church, organization or your individual role is shifting or moving from wartime to peacetime or vice versa, you must begin making some hard changes in your leadership style if you are to continue delivering the same kind of effective results. When all is said and done, it all comes down to the results you achieve. This is the primary reason losing coaches in major sports are canned when the going gets tough. The team owner knows it's easier to terminate the coach than a whole squad of "overpaid" professional athletes. So, as a leader, begin thinking wartime/peacetime. It forms the initial step towards leadership that is highly adaptable to your ever-changing role or responsibility.

Practical Examples/Illustrations

When John Swearingen of Standard Oil, who at the time was retired, made a comeback as CEO of Continental Illinois National Bank and Trust Company of Chicago, at that point the 6th largest bank in the nation, found the bank just a couple of months away from going under —the wartime scenario. Swearingen required every manager there, including me, who at the time was a Supervisor in the Distribution Services Department at CINB, to follow his exact plan with precision; outside the core mission of survival, there was to be no room for any "rogue" or individual pursuits. And did he succeed?! The successful Chemical Bank secured the holding company and is now quite profitable as the revitalized Bank of America.

On the other hand, as Google had already achieved global search market dominance, the management encouraged peacetime innovation by making it possible and even requiring each Google employee to spend at least 20% of their time on new personal projects.

Winston Churchill, the British Prime Minister, was a fantastic communicator and an exceptional wartime leader. His style of leadership greatly inspired the people of Britain throughout the war, lifting the nation's morale. He was hugely effective when it came to rallying the entire nation to one cause: survival.

Churchill, at the same time, gives us an excellent case study of what can potentially happen when you are unable to adapt your leadership style to a changing environment. His proven success as a wartime leader failed during the post-war environment of inclusive peacetime politics. In the era of the freshly minted President Donald Trump, however, that is a subject for another time.

Bottom line

Leaders need to know whether their business is at war or at peace. And to state the truth, most times, if you practice the concepts of Teach Tell and Train, as outlined throughout this publication, you will have a pretty good grasp of your personal status. Where we fail as managers/leaders is that often, we don't connect the dots regarding our style of leadership. Simply put, we make it up as we go along without having a concrete plan of action.

Though they are quite different, peacetime and wartime management techniques, when used in the proper context, can and will be highly effective. The bottom line is that a wartime manager or CEO does not resemble a peacetime manager or CEO. To be a truly effective leader, from this writer's perspective, you need to be adaptive to both styles of leadership. I put a simple catchphrase on the board, which my business mentor uttered, Mr. H. Craig Jones, when I taught my first business class at Concordia University in River Forest, Illinois, many years ago: ***"The whole is always greater than the sum of the individual parts."*** I still believe it today and so should you.

CHAPTER 6
The 80/20 Principle in Ministry

A Message to Pastors

The 80/20 Principle, also called the Pareto Principle, was named after Italian economist Vilfredo Pareto, who observed in 1906 that 80% of the land in Italy was owned by 20% of the population. This business concept has evolved and generally states that in any occupational activity, 20% of the investment results in 80% of the return. The leadership of any business/organization must decide if they want to invest in the 20% to make it the best that the 20% can be to undergird the return that the 20% is achieving or if they want to invest in the 80% to try and make that part more productive. That same 80/20 principle is true in ministry today as well. Therefore, church leaders face a similar decision. Does the leadership focus on equipping and supporting the 20% of those who are getting significant ministry accomplished? Or does the church leadership try to pull the 80% of those not achieving much in ministry along so that they can see a higher return from those 80%? Because ministry is different than business, there may be a time to focus on each section. You want to continue to grow those who are seeing great ministry results because there is always room for improvement and deeper discipleship. And, you don't want to give up on those who are not there yet because God may do work in them to mature them to where they are a significant benefit to ministry and are seeing more impressive spiritual returns from their ministry investment. But, understanding how the 80/20 Principle will affect the church helps in knowing how to best allocate funds, time, and equipping resources.

20% of Members Do 80% of the Ministry

The good news is that any church, for the most part, is comprised of imperfect people on a mission to better themselves. The bad news surfaces when one starts looking objectively at the people who are involved in the active organization, administration, and sweat equity of the church; they will notice that the same people tend to show up at the different outreach opportunities, at the fellowships within the congregation, and in the various leadership roles. When thinking about a new area of ministry and who can help make that new ministry happen, your mind will go immediately to those people who are already plugged into other pieces of what the church is doing. The mentality remains: If you want to get something done, ask people who are already busy because they are the ones who are willing to work to achieve what needs to be done. Those who are not already busy are probably not busy because they do not want to be doing much anyway. Attention should be specified here because jealousy power can creep in among the "do-nothing crowd" that may reason: "This or that positive recognition should be offered up to me!"

Church leadership must show caution because it is easy to overwork those who are willing to put in the perspiration in the form of blood, sweat and tears of ministry. Those who are always willing to help must find times to be ministered to and taught as well. My pastor, Apostle Mark A. Henton, is known for calling out individuals who have put forth a stellar effort and justly recognize them for a job...well done! No one can continually give without needing their own heart and soul replenished and refreshed. If you constantly drain the 20%, you will see them burn out and lose their effectiveness and enthusiasm in ministry. This writer is currently involved with many leadership roles, such as The Women's Forum (sponsored by the men of the church), The Men's General Assembly, The Emergency Response Team, the Pastors Liaison and the President of the Men's Department, to name some of the vital connections that have linked me to the ministry, still constantly finding ways to mimic the pastors initiative by rewarding those among the 20 as Man of the Month; Man of the Year and a "Sports Fellowship" event at least once a calendar quarter. It is imperative that we know those who labor among us and reward/recognize them for that service!!!

Church leadership should never give up on the other 80%. As you disciple them and see their walks with the Lord growing, you will have the opportunity to plug them in and see them become useful for ministry. You can equip the saints for the work of the ministry, even the 80% who are not doing much (see Ephesians 4:11-12).

In Exodus, Moses, who has been lauded throughout this book, had to learn how to utilize people in ministry. But, when he was calling men to help him in judging the disputes of the people, Moses took Jethro's advice and called capable men who loved the Lord (see Exodus 18). Rather than looking for men not doing anything, Moses recruited the men who had already shown some ability to lead. Then Moses assigned them different levels of responsibility. Some of the 20% of the Israelites came alongside Moses to help in the ministry to the people.

20% of the Members Give 80% of the Money

Amazingly, most churches are similar to each other. They may be in different places. They may be reaching a different type of people. They may be older, established churches or newer church plants. But, in many ways, they are very comparable. One similarity that is true for the clear majority of churches is that 80% of the offerings received come from about 20% of the people.

In some cases, this comes from a disparity of income. The better-off people will have the capability to give more than those who do not make as much money or are surviving the forces of the inner city on a fixed income. But often, the lack of giving reveals more of a heart issue than a finance issue. One of the last things to grow in young disciples and newly minted ministers is the consistency in giving. Some members will give more than a tithe. Other members will give consistently and substantially, but it may not be a full tithe. As a rule, most members will give a small amount on an inconsistent basis.

One major way to grow the giving in the church is to teach and allow the Lord to change the hearts of the 80% who are merely giving God a "tip." They are just giving a nominal amount to the work of the Kingdom, mainly because they have not been taught, or have not responded to the teaching, of what God calls the Christian to do as being a good steward. Church leadership must continually teach that God owns everything that believers have because He has given it to them. But as more people are learning how to give, new people will be coming in who have not learned how to give unto the Lord yet. So, even as the church has more givers, the 80/20 rule of church giving will probably still apply. It is a never-ending process of teaching godly stewardship to those you are entrusted to you as a leader. Church leaders must find a way to impart unto their membership, not to consume their ***seed!***

20% of the Ministry Efforts Result in 80% of the Ministry Effectiveness

One last aspect of the 80/20 principle applies to the impact that certain ministries and activities within the church are making. Once again, you will see 80% of the results in ministry coming from 20% of the specific items that are on the church calendar. In this case, making that 20 % of the events become as great as they can leads to more results in ministry than trying to improve the 80% of the events that are just rolling along. Solid leadership will work at removing the most ineffective ministry events so that they are not taking resources from the most effective aspects of ministry. However, some churches have difficulty letting go of ministry efforts that have been around for any length of time at all. When an analysis is done on the church calendar, most churches will find that new families, new Christians, and growing disciples are coming from about 20% of the ministry activity. Focus on those things to improve the ministry. If possible, remove some of the other things that are weighing down the ministry.

Rather than being frustrated by the 80/20 Principle, use the knowledge to improve ministry effectiveness, ministry leaders, and ministry funds. By concentrating on the things that are successful in ministry, you can continue to grow the ministry and the people involved in ministry. Learn how to work smarter, not harder. The 80/20 Principle will help you do that.

CHAPTER 7
Volunteer Lives Matter

My graduate thesis at National-Louis University in Evanston, Illinois, some time ago was titled ***Successful Fundraising in a Not-for-profit Organization.*** My intention in this chapter is to draw upon my success as Executive Director of the From Boys To Men Network Foundation, a 501 © 3 not-for-profit foundation that I founded in 1995 with the intention of improving the lives of inner-city African American males. An entire chapter was devoted to attracting and maintaining enthusiastic volunteers. While some observers say the tenets of my research were impressive, it was largely rooted in my efforts to apply the information I had gathered through a multitude of assignments in the helping ministries. The Church is no different when it comes to those rendering and requesting service(s). The Church has to be, from my perspective, the largest volunteer organization in the world. Although we will apply principles here that are designed specifically for a ministry application, leaders of any organization or community endeavor can feel its usefulness. For the work of the Lord and the ministry to continue, volunteers must pour their lives and efforts into the work of the church. For the places of worship to thrive, they must find ways to applaud and appreciate the numerous volunteers who make a ministry happen. Church leaders must be intentional and consistent in showing how much the volunteers are valued and appreciated.

One of the difficulties in encouraging volunteers is that church leaders see the best, most faithful, most devoted volunteers all the time, as was discussed with the 80/20 rule last chapter. Unless care is taken, you can look right past those church members who are making the most productive ministry happen. When Jesus went back to His hometown of Nazareth, the people there questioned Jesus' ability to do anything because they had known Him and His family His entire life. They were so familiar with Jesus that they missed how special Jesus was. Jesus said it this way:

57 And they took offense at him. But Jesus said to them, "A prophet is not without honor except in his hometown and his own household." 58 And he did not do many mighty works there because of their unbelief. (Matthew 13:57-58, NIV).

You can easily miss those most dedicated volunteers because they are constantly right in front of you. If you overlook them and forget to appreciate them, you could easily lose them as volunteers.

Here are some areas that will help you show the gratitude to volunteers that they deserve. If leadership embraces these practices, volunteers will be more effective in ministry and more likely to continue to invest time, energy and finances in ministry.

1. **<u>Teach</u> volunteers to care about people.**

- *Know them.*

Each volunteer has unique situations going on in life. One has a sick parent who needs care. Another is in the middle of a job transition. Another has a child who is running from the Lord. And still another one is experiencing the joy of a baby on the way. Each person needs you to know what is going on in life so that you communicate that each one is valuable to you as a person, not as a person filling a spot.

- ***Spend time with them.***

The only way to get to know someone in that kind of way is to spend time with them. As often as you can, in the confines of time and appropriateness, spend time with individuals and the entire volunteer team when you can. The only way to grow in knowing them is to spend time with them. Carve out that time to grow to know your team.

- ***Recognize they have life going on outside of volunteering.***

Give your team some slack. When conflicts come up, let the team members know that you understand, that you are there for them, and that you want to help them in any way that you can. If your response is one of frustration, you will alienate your volunteers. If your response is one of love and empathy, you will connect with your team.

Do you know the real people who are the volunteers at your church?

2. <u>Tell</u> them as workers.

- ***Equip them.***

Your volunteers must be taught how to be effective in ministry. There are ministry skills that need to be refined and ministry principles that need to be understood for the most effective ministry to occur. The only way your volunteers will grow in those areas is for you to teach them and have others teach them how to do ministry.

- ***Invest in them.***

Let your volunteers know by what they see that you and the church are willing to invest time, energy, and money into making the volunteers better in ministry. Calendar training events. This shows that you see the importance of ministry time being spent on volunteers. Bring in speakers to equip your team or take your team to conferences with the church paying the way. This investment of funds shows that the church values the volunteers and the ministry they are doing.

- ***Tell volunteers who the group mediator is in your ministry and be quick to respond to volunteer complaints of the 20 percenters that the 80 percent group targets because of their loyalty and dedication. Unfortunately, every one of your volunteers won't be on the same page at the same time. Some will press their way simply for the glamour of the "spotlight." Do you equip your volunteers to perform the ministry tasks that you are asking them to do?***

3. <u>Train</u> them as co-laborers.

- ***Communicate with them.***

If your volunteers are going to feel like they are a vital part of the leadership team, you must work hard to communicate what is going on and when things are going to happen. If the volunteers are in the dark about certain ministry items, they feel like you don't trust them with the information or you don't value them enough to inform them what is going on. Communication speaks importance to those receiving it.

- ***Respect their time and opportunity cost.***

Do not waste the time of your volunteers. Opportunity cost is the time you invest as a volunteer that you could be doing something else. When you have a meeting with your volunteers, make sure the meeting is important to what they are trying to accomplish in ministry. Start on time. Be prepared. Let them know that you have done what you need to do to be ready for your time with them. Side note: No productive meeting should last longer than an hour. Always respect the value of time. Your volunteers will respond accordingly.

- ***Say "thanks" often.***

This saying "thanks" may be done in a formal way, such as a banquet, dinner or public acknowledgment. These immense ways of thanking your volunteers are important. But, also remember to say "thanks" often in your conversations with them. Let them hear from your heart that you are grateful for the investment they are making in the work of the kingdom of God. Written notes provide another great way to express appreciation for what the volunteers are doing. A few "thanks" go a long way in expressing value for those who sacrifice to make ministry happen.

- ***Connect what they do to the gospel.***

Remind the volunteers often that they are making an eternal impact for the glory of God. People are being saved because of what they do. Christians are growing in Christ because of the ministry that the volunteers perform. Each volunteer is handling responsibilities that matter in the big picture, no matter how insignificant the part they play may seem. It takes everyone working together to positively impact the ministry in the most effective way.

Do you treat your volunteers as co-laborers in the work of the kingdom?

In ministry, we can become so focused on the goal of the project that we become desensitized to the end result, causing us to lose sight of the people who are involved along the way. To properly minister to your volunteers and to motivate your volunteers to properly minister to others, they must feel appreciated. As a church leader, it is your responsibility to show appreciation to your volunteers. Moses and Jethro dealt with this scenario often in the book of Exodus (Chapter 18). Don't miss the mark on that responsibility, or you will be conveying your department assignments as a well-meaning yet misguided Moses figure in ministry.

CHAPTER 8
Youth Leaders Rock!

Preparing the Next Generation for Leadership

Look at the next generation coming up. Think through some people in your church/ organization, as a matter of fact, by name. Did you consider enough people that you can count on one hand? That would actually be pretty good, depending on the size of the church/organization and the scope of your mission statement. How ready will these persons be to lead in the future? How ready are they to lead now? What are the current leadership and the church administration doing to prepare them to step into the leadership roles that will undoubtedly become available as time passes? If a leadership deficiency occurs, it is not the fault of the generation that is struggling to lead. The blame falls square on the previous generation that failed to prepare them for leadership roles and the responsibility that goes with it. The church is not static (standing still); consequently, it must work now to prepare those who will be among the leaders of tomorrow by working purposely and passionately to prepare them to lead. This writer has been blessed to have more than a fair share of mentors in my youth who have steered me back on course. My labor in the vineyard as an Assistant Choir Manager, New Converts' Instructor, Youth Director, Sunday School Teacher and Youth Pastor have proven as valuable tools for this one-time ministerial apprentice and have yielded much fruit as this book allows an opportunity for me to give back!

How To Prepare

Working with that next generation of leaders takes some specific actions that will result in raising leaders who are equipped to handle the difficult task of leadership in a way that will carry the church and propel the church into what God has planned for His kingdom. Here are some ways to pass on leadership skills to prepare the rising leaders:

1. Teach

Preparation starts with teaching the next generation everything that God wants us to know and do. They must learn from God's Word who God is, the salvation He accomplishes through Christ, and how God wants us to share that message with others. They must be growing disciples of Christ. Unless we teach these rising leaders what they need to know, we cannot expect them to lead in a way that honors God and impacts others. They cannot know what they have not been taught. Teach the next generation of leaders the foundational truths of God.

2. Tell

After teaching them about who God is, we need to tell them and show them, sometimes by example, how that foundational knowledge translates into ministry for today and into the future. Growing in ministry happens because we speak to this upcoming generation of the leadership skills that are needed today and will be needed tomorrow. These leadership skills are constantly changing as the world around us is changing. But, the principles of leadership will stay the change. The next generation of leaders will be ministering in a very different world than we have today. We must tell them how to grow as leaders so they can impact the world that they will face.

3. Train

As we teach and tell, we must also train younger leaders. Training comes as they walk alongside us and watch us do ministry. This allows them to see firsthand, as Pastor E. R. Allen, my former pastor and mentor, instructed me as a Youth Pastor what was being done to positively impact the Church, Christ Bible Center, Chicago, Illinois; I was also serving as the Assistant Pastor. Never did I shy away from an opportunity to learn by doing. Pastor E. R. would always explain why "this" or "that" was the best course of action, then step back and allow me to see the bigger picture, thus allowing me to choose the best course of action. Some mistakes will be made during this process, however, none that can't be corrected by common sense and deductive reasoning. We, as co-laborers in ministry, can offer guidance and counsel to followers who will or have already encountered issues beyond their control. We let them lead out, but we are right there to assist when they need it and critique or correct in love when a better way exists to lead. Finally, we can launch them into ministry and let them fly on their own (not to be confused with flying by the seat of their pants). This pattern of letting them watch while we do, letting them do while we watch, and then letting them do while we equip someone else will help to create the most resilient and effective leaders.

Why Prepare

By thinking through why it is important to prepare the upcoming generation, we will be more motivated to make it happen. We must see the value in having a group of leaders coming after us who will be ready to take the church to where God wants it to go. Here are three main reasons for equipping younger leaders:

1. This Helps the Current Church

The primary reason that it is worth pouring into those who are coming behind us is that we can have more help in accomplishing ministry now. When more leaders are trained, those leaders can be used in ministry in the life of the church today. This will take some of the burdens of ministry off the current leadership. They will have more people to spread the ministry over. As these younger leaders emerge, the current leadership can focus on other aspects of ministry because they have invested so much in the next generations of leaders who are ready to help provide ministry today. When current leadership has more leaders to use, ministry is more effective and less burdensome for those leading out now. A note of caution is that some reluctant leaders with hidden agendas or ulterior motives won't always be quick to turn over the "baton" of leadership when circumstances permit or warrant; however, an effective leader/Pastor will know when to intercede for the success of the cause.

2. This Taps Into the Next Generation

Another reason for investing in the next generation of leaders is that the church will be blessed today. We tend to think of our children, teenagers, and young adults as the church of tomorrow. Though that is true, we cannot miss the fact that they can also be the church of today. Who is going to be effective in reaching teenagers today? Other teenagers who are on fire for the Lord. Who can make an impact on ministering to young adults today? Young adults who know Christ and are living for Him. One glaring personal example comes to mind, having served in the Chicago Public Schools as an Assistant Choir Manager by way of an after-school incentives program to keep youth engaged between the hours of 3:00 pm and 7:00m, a time when idle minds drift into bewilderment. If you, as a Christian, have a disdain for all genres of music, with the exception of Christian/Gospel music, you will have a problem seeking to lead the church of tomorrow. I had no preconceived notion that kids singing for two hours after school would change the world; however, it did provide me an example to *hear* them, literally and figuratively and vice versa. This was an opportunity for discipleship...pure and simple. The younger generation is not just the church of the future. They can be the church of today. Let's grow them in Christ. Let's grow them in leadership. Let's watch what God does through them *today* in the church.

3. This Helps the Future Church

Undoubtedly, the most visible return on the investment of the next generation is the future church. As leaders, it is our responsibility to ensure that tomorrow's church is ready to pass along the truth of the gospel to all who need to hear God's truth. We cannot have the church diminish because we did not take seriously our calling to equip those who are coming behind us. The church of the future will desperately need strong leaders who will come from the younger generation that is coming up now. The work of the kingdom cannot afford for us to fail to train the leaders of tomorrow.

As we have continually referenced in this book, In Exodus 18, Moses learns the lesson from Jethro and gives us an example of how to train the younger generation. He set different leaders over different amounts of people. Certainly, as someone became proficient at making good decisions and showing proper judgment over a few people, Moses would elevate them to having more responsibility for more people. The model still works. With our younger generation of leaders, we can give them smaller responsibilities and teach them how to handle them. Then, as they grow in experience and confidence, we can put them over more areas of ministry and grow them in the responsibilities where they are leading.

We will be doing a great disservice to the Lord, His kingdom, and the church if we do not train the younger generation to lead. Let's make sure that we are leaving behind strong leaders who will make a difference in the church as they follow the Lord and serve Him. Let's be diligent as servants to train up the next generation of leaders. Solomon said it best in the book of Proverbs (26:2 NIV): ***"Start children off on the way they should go, and even when they are old, they will not turn from it."***

THEME SONG

Moses: Teach, Tell and Train (Hip-Hop Rap)

TriDreams Productions

Copyright © 2017

Stanley G Buford

CHORUS (Teach)

Moses, what are we doing

We are in the desert, man

I thought you told us you would get us to the promised land

Man, I need some food; teach us as you oughtta

I'm thirsty like you won't believe, and I could use some water

we, the kids of Israel, yeah, we, the sons and daughters

We love to seek; you love to teach!

ISRAELITE (Tell)

Moses, what are we doing

I saw you lift the seas

I need a break. This was a mistake; it is 100 degrees

I know you talk to God

I know you brought the plagues

you said we'd get to the promised land, but my friends are dead

kids have lost their parents

parents have lost their kids

I'm questioning if God is there because if he were, he wouldn't do this

Man, I need some water

I haven't seen it in weeks

the people built an idol because they think your methods stink

Moses, we all love you

Tell us our God is still enough

maybe if we pray some more, we'll get there in under a month

I saved a spot for you

I hope you won't be angry

this is the way now come and let us pray

Your body language speaks of God: "Please do all I say!"

MOSES (Train)

first of all, son, I did not lift up the seas

that was God give him credit and give none to me

yes, I talked to God, and Jethro helped me too

now it's raining manna because God provided food

then y'all wanted water, so again, I knocked

and God answered, and we got some when I hit a rock

but God has his rules

they're called the 10 commandments

You all already broke one when you made the idol when you panicked

yeah, we're stranded on this planet. I know that you all feel abandoned

but we're standing with commandments, and if we do as He's demanded

we'll get to the promised land, man, you all, just please be unrestrained

The object of this journey is to Teach, Tell, and Train

AFTERWARD

What Would Moses Do?

Bible Trivia: Moses as a character is awe-inspiring. He is the ultimate image of a leader. He is a grand and ambitious bible symbol. Viewed up close, we see him as we do ourselves; we all, from time to time, appear as somewhat reluctant leaders or managers of people trying desperately to learn to lead per God's direction. That is why the cover image was chosen for this book- it reflects the episodes in this writer's life. Leading by example presently with the knowledge of those on whose shoulders we stand, yet with a view to the future.

Moses was adept at modeling the way by setting an example from side to side, behaving in ways that were reliable with common core values.

Cover Art: Peipei

As a Leader, Moses inspired others in these subject areas:

- ❖ Respected and feared: (Exodus 33:8)
- ❖ Faith: (Numbers 10:29 De 9:1-3 Hebrews 11:23-28)
- ❖ Called the man of God: (Deuteronomy 33:1)
- ❖ God spoke as a man to his friend (Exodus 33:11)
- ❖ Magnified of God: (Exodus 19:9 Nu 14:12-20 Deuteronomy 9:13-29)
- ❖ Fairness: (Numbers 11:29)
- ❖ Meekness: (Exodus 14:13, 14; 15:24, 25; 16:2, 3, 7, 8 Numbers 12:3; 16:4-11)
- ❖ Obedience: (Exodus 7:6; 40:16, 19, 21)
- ❖ Apathetic: (Numbers 14; 12-20 De 9:13-29 Ex 32:30)

QUIZ

**Think you're familiar enough with Moses'
exploits in the bible?**

Try this simple quiz:

Moses Bible Trivia

1.   As Moses was watching the people at their hard labor,
whom did he see beating a Hebrew?
(Exodus 2:11)
   a.   An Egyptian
   b.   Pharaoh
   c.   A Hebrew woman
   d.   Pharaoh's daughter

2.   After killing the person who was beating a Hebrew,
where did Moses hide the body? (Exodus 2:12)
   a.   In a forest
   b.   In the Nile River
   c.   In bulrushes
   d.   In the sand

3.   What did Moses think when he heard the response of
the fighting man? (Exodus 2:14)
   a.   "This man thinks I am a ruler."
   b.   "What I did must have become known."
   c.   "This man thinks I am a judge."
   d.   "I just killed this man, too."

4.   What was said when the baby was named "Moses"?
(Exodus 2:10)
   a.   "I drew him out of the water."
   b.   "He will be a great leader."
   c.   "He is the son of the princess."

    d. "Out of slavery into royalty."

5. What did Moses ask a Hebrew who was fighting with another Hebrew? (Exodus 2:13)

    a. "Why are you hitting your fellow Hebrew?"
    b. "Must I kill you as I did the Egyptian?"
    c. "Who is your father?"
    d. "Why are you fighting with each other?"

6. What was the name given to Moses' son when Moses said, "I have become an alien in a foreign land"? (Exodus2:22)

    a. Reuel
    b. Levi
    c. Jethro
    d. Gershom

7. Where did Moses go to live when Pharaoh tried to kill him? (Exodus 2:15)

    a. His Hebrew mother's home
    b. Midian
    c. Canaan
    d. The palace of Pharaoh's daughter

8. What was the name of the daughter Reuel gave to be Moses' wife? (Exodus 2:21)

    a. Leah
    b. Zipporah
    c. Rachel
    d. Dinah

9. Who did Moses encounter at a well in Midian? (Exodus 2:15-18)

    a. The seven daughters of a priest named Reuel
    b. A Samaritan woman
    c. The daughter of Laban
    d. Moses did not visit a well in Midian

10. To whom did God send Moses to bring the Israelites out of Egypt? (Exodus 3:10)
    a. The Levites
    b. The High Priest
    c. Pharaoh
    d. Pharaoh's daughter

11. Why did Reuel's daughters need Moses to rescue them? (Exodus 2:17)
    a. They fell into the well
    b. The sheep were running away
    c. Shepherds had driven them away
    d. Their father refused to help them

12. When speaking to the Israelites, who specifically was Moses to say had sent him?
(Exodus 3:13-14)
    a. Jesus
    b. The God of your fathers
    c. I Am
    d. The LORD

13. What did Moses do when God announced who he was? (Exodus 3:6)
    a. Hid his face because he was afraid
    b. His face because he was ashamed
    c. Turned and ran
    d. Fell to his knees

14. What was Moses' response when God called to him from within the burning bush?
(Exodus 3:4)
    a. "Who are you?"
    b. "I am unworthy - how can I reply to you?"
    c. "Woe to me! I am ruined!"
    d. "Here I am."

15. What was Moses instructed to remove because he was standing on holy ground?
(Exodus 3:5)

      a. His cloak
      b. His sandals (shoes)
      c. His head covering
      d. His belt

Moses Bible Trivia: Answer Key

1. A. An Egyptian

2. D. In the sand

3. B. "What I did must have become known."

4. A. "I drew him out of the water."

5. A. Why are you hitting your fellow Hebrew?"

6. D. Gershom

7. B. Midian

8. B. Zipporah

9. A. The seven daughters of a priest named Reuel

10. C. Pharaoh

11. C. Shepherds has driven them away

12. C. I Am

13. A. His face, because he was afraid

14. D. "Here I am."

15. B. His sandals (shoes)

REFERENCE LIST

David, B. (2009). Leadership in organizations: There is a difference between Leaders and Managers.

Beall, Anne E. "Body language speaks." communication world (March/April 2004): 18–20.

Bickerstaff Glover, R. (2015). Handshake Etiquette. Retrieved March 23, 2015, from http://etiquette.about.com/od/RelationshipEtiquette/a/GreetingEtiquette.htm

"Examples of body language." your dictionary, n.d. web. 19 January 2015. <http://examples.yourdictionary.com/examples-of-body-language.html>.

Knapp, m, l., and j.a. Hall. Nonverbal communication in human interaction. 5th Ed. Fort Worth, TX: Wadsworth, 2002.

Konnellan, Thomas K. "Great expectations, great results." hrmagazine (June 2003): 155–158.

Marr, Bernard. "The 15 Biggest Body Language Mistakes to Watch Out For" Linked In., (July 7, 2014).

Navarro, J. (2013). The Art of Handshaking. Retrieved March 23, 2015 from https://www.psychologytoday.com/blog/spycatcher/201307/the-art-handshaking

Pease, Allen and Barbara. "The Definitive Book of Body Language" Bantam Books, New York: 2006.

Ribbens, Geoff, and Richard Thompson. Understanding body language. Barron's educational series, 2001.

Cuddy, Amy TED. 2007. TED Ideas Worth Spreading. New York: TED. http://www.ted.com/

Goman, Carol Kinsey. 2008. The nonverbal advantage secrets and science of body language at work. San Francisco, Calif: Berrett-Koehler;
Publishers.http://www.books24x7.com/marc.asp bookid=23476

ABOUT THE AUTHOR

In a previous book directed to those who take parenting seriously in the Urban Canters of America, Former President Barack Obama remarked: "Thank you for your interesting book on parenting."

Stanley G. Buford was born in Chicago, Illinois. He studied at Illinois State University and holds master's degrees from National-Louis University in Management/Human Resource Development and DePaul University in Curriculum Development. He has worked as a "results-driven" teacher in Chicago Public Schools, the Archdioceses of Chicago and as a Charter School Employee.

Stanley has appeared as a guest on the nationally televised show, "Heartbeat of America," in a frank discussion concerning challenges to climbing corporate and educational ladders. He owns and operates a state-certified management consulting business, Terkat Consultants Inc. He has been quoted in news articles while lecturing at schools such as Northwestern, DePaul and the University of Illinois on a variety of contemporary issues. An avid marathoner, actor, playwright and visionary.

Stanley has served as the Program Director of the School Partnerships Program, a school improvement project at DePaul University. He has also served as an adjunct faculty member at Concordia University. He founded his mentoring program, From Boys To Men Network Foundation, in 1991 to improve the quality of life for school-age boys in Chicago's inner city. In this non-fiction book, The Moses Principle of Leadership: Teach, Tell & Train, Stanley combines 3 critical elements of time-tested procedures practiced by Moses and Jethro from the Bible. Teach, Tell, &Train will enrich all practitioners, whether in business or personal relationships. This work is a follow-up to his Amazon.com bestseller ***_Not All Teachers Are Parents, But All Parents Are Teachers!_***